SEATTLE SEAHAWKS

BY ALEX MONNIG

Published by The Child's World®
1980 Lookout Drive • Mankato, MN 56003-1705
800-599-READ • www.childsworld.com

Acknowledgments
The Child's World®: Mary Berendes, Publishing Director
Red Line Editorial: Editorial direction
The Design Lab: Design
Amnet: Production

Design Element: Dean Bertoncelj/Shutterstock Images
Photographs ©: Patric Schnider/AP Images, cover;
William Purnell/Icon Sportswire, 5; G. Newman
Lowrance/AP Images, 7; Vernon Biever/AP Images, 9;
Contra Costa Times/ZumaPress/Icon Sportswire, 11;
Stephen Brashear/AP Images, 13; Greg Trott/AP Images,
14–15; Tom Reed/AP Images, 17; Kevin Larkin/AP
Images, 19; John Froschauer/AP Images, 21; Jesse Beals/
Icon SMI/Corbis, 23; Aaron M. Sprecher/AP Images, 25;
William Purnell/Icon Sportswire/Corbis, 27; Kevin Reece/
Icon Sportswire, 29

ISBN 9781634070171
LCCN 2014959722

Printed in the United States of America
Mankato, MN
July, 2015
PA02265

ABOUT THE AUTHOR

Alex Monnig is a freelance journalist from St. Louis, Missouri, who now lives in Sydney, Australia. He has traveled across the world to cover sporting events in China, India, Singapore, New Zealand, and Scotland. No matter where he is, he always makes time to keep up to date with his favorite teams from his hometown.

TABLE OF CONTENTS

GO, SEAHAWKS!

The Seattle Seahawks did not win a Super Bowl for 37 years. Many of those years were tough. Then, coaches Mike Holmgren and Pete Carroll turned the Seahawks around. Seattle won its first Super Bowl after the 2013 season. The fans loved it. Seahawks fans are considered the loudest in football. That gives the team a great home-field advantage. Let's meet the Seahawks.

Quarterback Russell Wilson (3) hands off the ball to running back Marshawn Lynch (24) during a game against the Kansas City Chiefs on November 16, 2014.

WHO ARE THE SEAHAWKS?

The Seattle Seahawks play in the National Football **League** (NFL). They are one of 32 teams in the NFL. The NFL includes the American Football Conference (AFC) and the National Football Conference (NFC). The winner of the NFC plays the winner of the AFC in the Super Bowl. The Seahawks play in the West Division of the NFC. The Seahawks have played in the Super Bowl three times. They won the second time.

Seahawks quarterback Russell Wilson celebrates after leading his team to victory in Super Bowl XLVIII on February 2, 2014.

WHERE THEY CAME FROM

In the 1970s, the NFL wanted to add two new teams. The Seahawks became one of them. They entered the NFL in 1976. The team was named in a fan contest. There were 1,741 different names suggested. In the end, Seahawks was chosen. The team has been in Seattle ever since. It made the playoffs just five times in its first 27 seasons. But the 2013 Seahawks finally won the Super Bowl on February 2, 2014.

Quarterback Jim Zorn tries to pass during the Seahawks' fifth straight loss on October 10, 1976.

WHO THEY PLAY

The Seahawks play 16 games each season. With so few games, each one is important. Every year, the Seahawks play two games against each of the other three teams in their division. Those teams are the Arizona Cardinals, San Francisco 49ers, and St. Louis Rams. The Seahawks also play six other NFC teams and four from the AFC. The 49ers and the Seahawks are big **rivals**. The Seahawks beat the 49ers in the 2013 NFC Championship Game.

Seahawks kicker Steven Hauschka (4) boots a field goal during the Seahawks' 23-17 win in the NFC Championship game on January 19, 2014.

WHERE THEY PLAY

Seahawks Stadium was built in 2002. It was renamed CenturyLink Field in 2011. It holds 67,000 fans. But the fans are so loud it sounds like there are even more. That is because CenturyLink Field was built to be loud. Sound usually rises into the sky. But many of the seats at CenturyLink are under cover. That keeps noise in. It also protects fans from rainy Seattle weather.

Fireworks shoot off before a November 23, 2014, game between the Seahawks and Arizona Cardinals at CenturyLink Field.

THE FOOTBALL FIELD

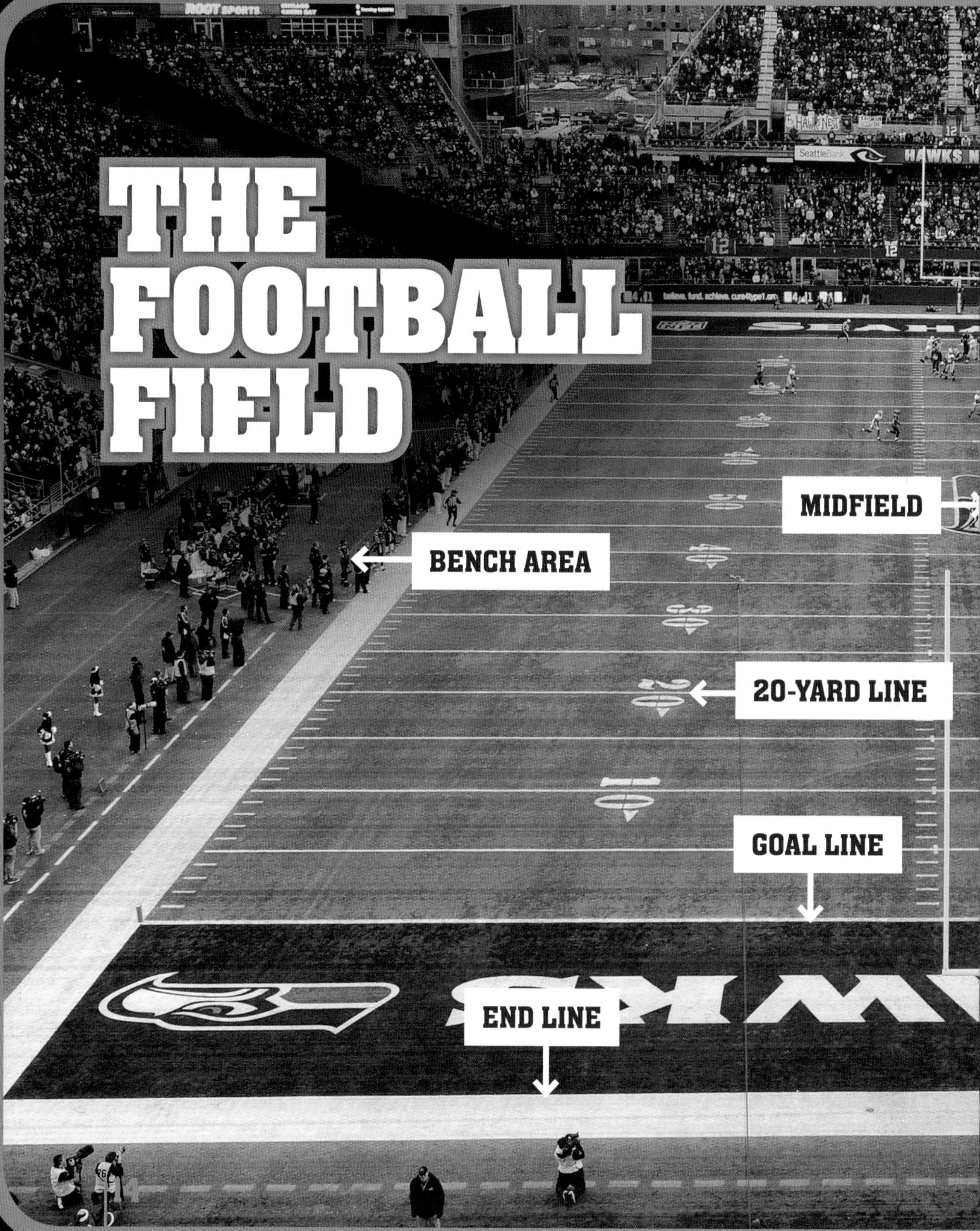

MIDFIELD

BENCH AREA

20-YARD LINE

GOAL LINE

END LINE

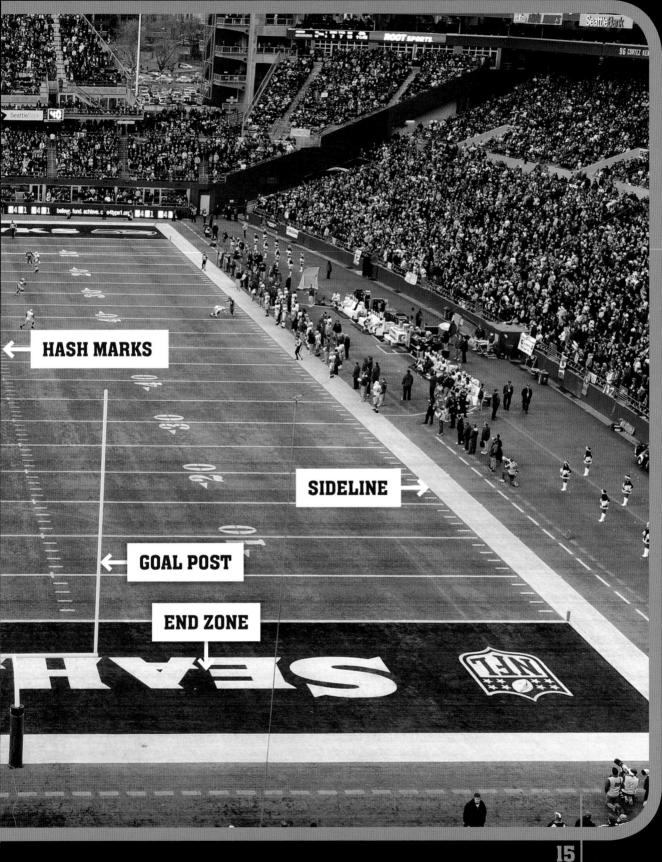

HASH MARKS

SIDELINE

GOAL POST

END ZONE

BIG DAYS

The Seahawks have had some great moments in their history. Here are three of the greatest:

1976—Wide receiver Steve Largent joined the team in a trade from the Houston Oilers. He became a legend and Seattle's best player. When he retired in 1989, he held NFL career records for catches (819), receiving yards (13,089), and **touchdown** catches (100).

2006—On January 1, running back Shaun Alexander scored his 28th touchdown of the 2005 season. That set a record. He also led the league with 1,880 rushing yards. Those totals earned him the **Most Valuable Player (MVP)** award. That season, the Seahawks went 13-3 and made it to the Super Bowl.

Receiver Steve Largent (80) runs after making a catch during a game against the Washington Redskins on September 28, 1986.

2014—The 2013 Seahawks finally won the Super Bowl on February 2, 2014. They defeated the Denver Broncos 43-8. Denver's **offense** had set many scoring records that season. But Seattle's **defense** kept the Broncos off the scoreboard for almost three quarters.

TOUGH DAYS

Football is a hard game. Even the best teams have rough games and seasons. Here are some of the toughest times in Seahawks history.

1979—In a game against the Los Angeles Rams, Seattle had minus-7 yards of total offense. That is the fewest in NFL history. It was not surprising they were **shut out** 24-0.

1992—The Seahawks had their worst season ever. They finished 2-14. That is the most losses in one season in team history. The Seahawks only scored 140 points all year.

2008—Coach Mike Holmgren left Seattle. He had led the team for ten years. The Seahawks made the

Seahawks quarterback Stan Gelbaugh (18) tries to escape from a sack during a game against the New York Giants on October 25, 1992.

playoffs six times under Holmgren. They had made the playoffs only four times in the 23 seasons before his arrival.

MEET THE FANS

Seahawks fans are known as the 12th Man. That is because they are so loud they act like an extra player on the field. Fans at a 2013 game against the New Orleans Saints set a world record for noise in an open-air stadium. The noise can make it hard for visiting teams to call plays. The Seahawks have honored fans by retiring jersey No. 12.

Seahawks fans celebrate as the Lombardi trophy comes to Seattle following the 2013 Seahawks' Super Bowl win.

HEROES THEN

Wide receiver Steve Largent missed only four games in his first 13 seasons in the NFL, from 1976 to 1988. The Steve Largent Award is given each year to the player who best represents the spirit, dedication, and integrity of the Seahawks. Defensive tackle Cortez Kennedy spent his entire career with Seattle. He was named the 1992 Defensive Player of the Year. He made the **Pro Bowl** eight times in his 11 seasons. Largent and Kennedy are in the Pro Football Hall of Fame. Shaun Alexander and quarterback Matt Hasselbeck teamed up in the 2000s. The Seahawks made the playoffs five times in seven years with Alexander and Hasselbeck.

Quarterback Matt Hasselbeck (8) passes to running back Shaun Alexander (37) on December 6, 2004.

HEROES NOW

Quarterback Russell Wilson chose football over baseball after college. It was a good choice. He beats teams by running and throwing the ball. Behind Wilson, the Seahawks made the Super Bowl after the 2013 and 2014 seasons. Defensive backs Richard Sherman, Earl Thomas, and Kam Chancellor fly around the field making plays. They are part of the "Legion of Boom" defense. Sherman is on the cover of the popular *Madden NFL 15* video game. He is only the third defensive player to receive that honor.

The Legion of Boom defensive backs celebrate during the Super Bowl on February 2, 2014.

GEARING UP

NFL players wear team uniforms. They wear helmets and pads to keep them safe. Cleats help them make quick moves and run fast. Some players wear extra gear for protection.

THE FOOTBALL

NFL footballs are made of leather. Under the leather is a lining that fills with air to give the ball its shape. The leather has bumps or "pebbles." These help players grip the ball. Laces help players control their throws. Footballs are also called "pigskins" because some of the first balls were made from pig bladders. Today they are made of leather from cows.

Quarterback Russell Wilson runs the ball during a 24-20 loss against the Kansas City Chiefs on November 6, 2014.

HELMET

SHOULDER PADS

THIGH PADS

KNEE PADS

FOOTBALL

LEATS

SPORTS STATS

 Here are some of the all-time career records for the Seattle Seahawks. All the stats are through the 2014 season.

INTERCEPTIONS

Dave Brown 50

Eugene Robinson 42

RUSHING YARDS

Shaun Alexander 9,429

Chris Warren 6,706

RECEPTIONS

Steve Largent 819

Brian Blades 581

TOTAL TOUCHDOWNS

Shaun Alexander 112

Steve Largent 101

SACKS

Jacob Green 97.5

Michael Sinclair 73.5

POINTS

Norm Johnson 810

Shaun Alexander 672

Seahawks quarterback Dave Krieg drops back to pass.

PASSING YARDS

Matt Hasselbeck 29,434

Dave Krieg 26,132

GLOSSARY

defense the unit of a football team that tries to keep the other team from scoring

league an organization of sports teams that compete against each other

Most Valuable Player (MVP) a yearly award given to the top player in the NFL

offense the unit of a football team that has the ball and tries to score points

Pro Bowl the NFL's All-Star game, in which the best players in the league compete

rivals teams whose games bring out the greatest emotion between the players and the fans on both sides

shut out when a team does not score any points

touchdown a play in which the ball is held in the other team's end zone, resulting in six points

FIND OUT MORE

IN THE LIBRARY

Carroll, Peter N., Yogi Roth, and Kristoffer A. Garin. *Win Forever: Live, Work, and Play Like a Champion*. New York: Portfolio, 2010.

Raible, Steve, and Mike Sando. *Tales from the Seattle Seahawks Sideline: A Collection of the Greatest Seahawks Stories Ever Told*. New York: Sports Publishing, 2012.

Turner, Mark Tye. *Notes from a 12 Man: A Truly Biased History of the Seattle Seahawks*. Seattle, WA: Sasquatch Books, 2009.

ON THE WEB

Visit our Web site for links about the Seattle Seahawks:
childsworld.com/links

Note to Parents, Teachers, and Librarians: We routinely verify our Web links to make sure they are safe and active sites. So encourage your readers to check them out!

INDEX